Adam Frost

THE EPIC BOOK OF EPICNESS

The world's most **EPIC FACTS**

BLOOMSBURY

LONDON NEW DELHI NEW YORK SYDNEY

To Anna and Eliza

Published 2015 by Bloomsbury Publishing Plc
50 Bedford Square, London, WC1B 3DP
www.bloomsbury.com
Bloomsbury is a registered trademark of Bloomsbury Publishing Plc

ISBN: 978-1-4088-6234-6

Produced for Bloomsbury Publishing Plc by Dutch&Dane
With thanks to Joseph Gwinn

Printed in China by Leo Paper Products, Heshan, Guangdong

1 3 5 7 9 10 8 6 4 2

All figures used in this book are believed to be the latest and most accurate figures at
the point of publication, unless the copy states otherwise. Where figures are estimates
or approximations, we have tried to make this clear. A selection of books and websites
we used for our facts can be found on the Sources page at the back of the book.

IN DEEP WATER

The Lake Argyle freshwater marathon involves swimming 60 kilometres across an enormous, crocodile-infested reservoir. How many crocs are in there, you ask..?

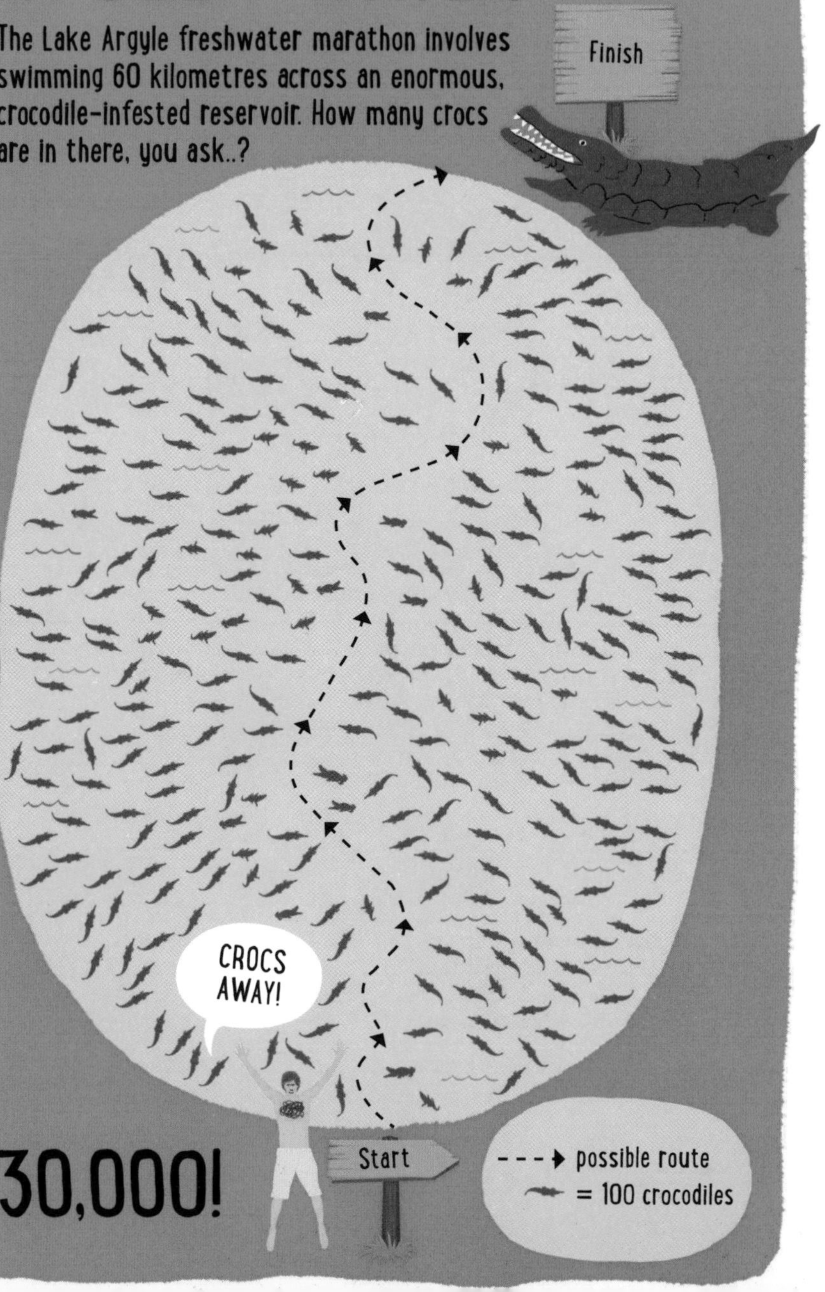

30,000!

DEAD SCARY

If all the dead people on Earth came back to life, how many would there be of THEM and how many of US?

ZOMBIES: 101 BILLION

HUMANS: 7 BILLION

I'm DYING for a bite.

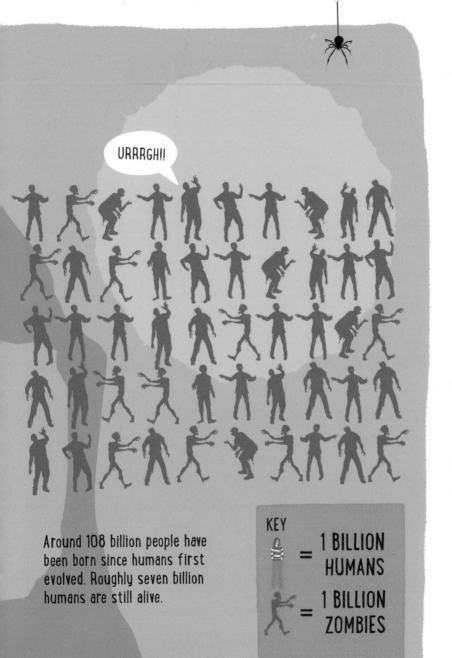

URRRGH!!

Around 108 billion people have been born since humans first evolved. Roughly seven billion humans are still alive.

KEY
= 1 BILLION HUMANS
= 1 BILLION ZOMBIES

SHARK ATTACK?

You're stuck on a desert island and you can see a shark's fin cutting through the water. But should you be worried?

Worry a lot

Tiger shark
Nicknamed 'the dustbin of the sea', this shark scoffs pretty much anything.

Great white
The largest of all sharks, with up to 300 razor-sharp teeth in its mouth.

YIKES!

Worry a bit

Oceanic whitetip
These sharks sometimes attack air crash survivors.

Blue shark
Blue sharks attack people rarely, but it does happen.

Uh-oh.

Don't worry

Zebra shark
These sharks are easy to spot (geddit?). They don't attack people though.

Pelagic thresher
A fast swimmer with a long tail, this shark feeds only on fish.

Whale shark
This shark is the biggest fish in the sea. It could swallow a person whole – but never has.

Basking shark
It's the second biggest fish – but the basking shark is completely harmless to people.

Zzzzz

IS ANYBODY OUT THERE?

It takes a while for messages to get to other planets. If you were talking to people on Venus, Mars, Jupiter or Neptune, how much could you say in an hour?

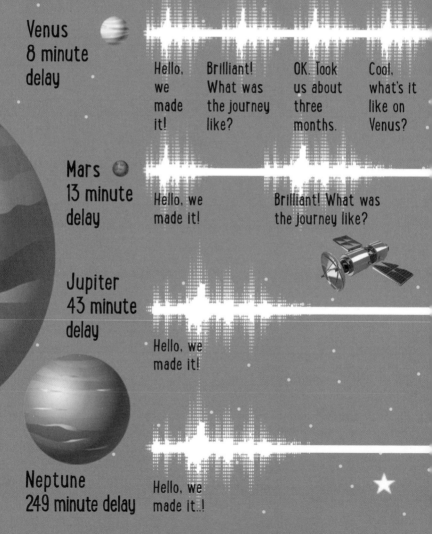

Venus
8 minute delay

Hello, we made it!

Brilliant! What was the journey like?

OK. Took us about three months.

Cool, what's it like on Venus?

Mars
13 minute delay

Hello, we made it!

Brilliant! What was the journey like?

Jupiter
43 minute delay

Hello, we made it!

Neptune
249 minute delay

Hello, we made it..!

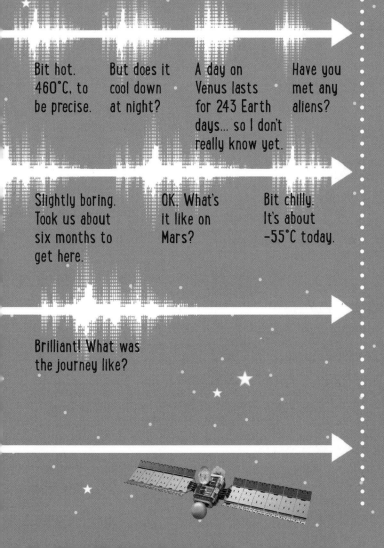

ONE HOUR

Bit hot. 460°C, to be precise.

But does it cool down at night?

A day on Venus lasts for 243 Earth days... so I don't really know yet.

Have you met any aliens?

Slightly boring. Took us about six months to get here.

OK. What's it like on Mars?

Bit chilly. It's about -55°C today.

Brilliant! What was the journey like?

DRIED UP OR WASHED OUT?

Most things, including human beings, contain a lot of water. But HOW much, exactly?

Egyptian mummy
0%
water

Cream cracker
5%
water

Loaf of bread
36%
water

Human being
65%
water

Potato
79%
water

Snail
80%
water

Grass
85%
water

Jellyfish
95%
water

IN A FLAP

How frequently do animals flap
their wings to stay in the air?

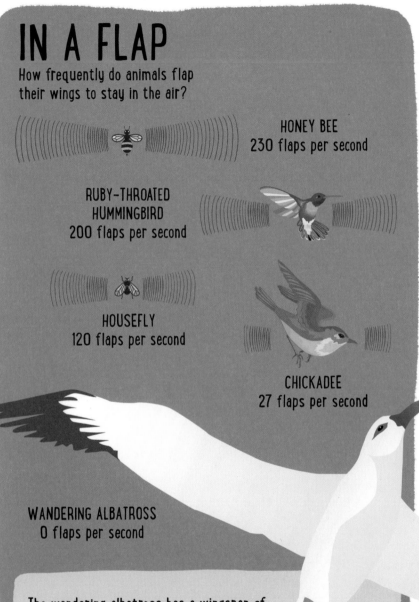

HONEY BEE
230 flaps per second

**RUBY-THROATED
HUMMINGBIRD**
200 flaps per second

HOUSEFLY
120 flaps per second

CHICKADEE
27 flaps per second

WANDERING ALBATROSS
0 flaps per second

The wandering albatross has a wingspan of
THREE METRES. It can glide on currents of air
for up to SIX DAYS without flapping its wings.

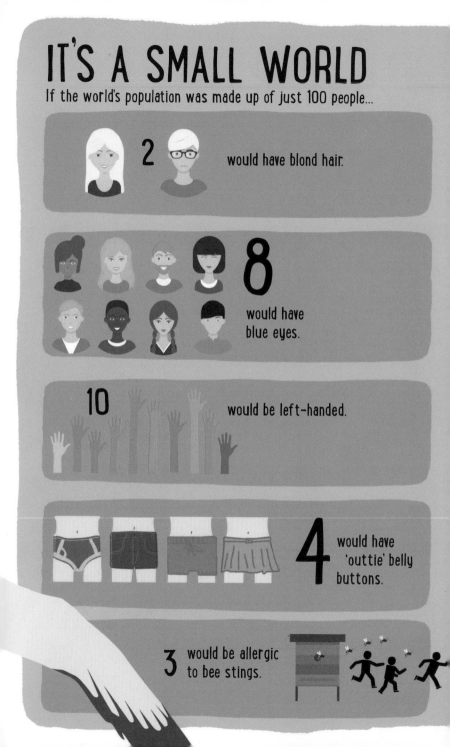

IT'S A SMALL WORLD

If the world's population was made up of just 100 people...

2 would have blond hair.

8 would have blue eyes.

10 would be left-handed.

4 would have 'outtie' belly buttons.

3 would be allergic to bee stings.

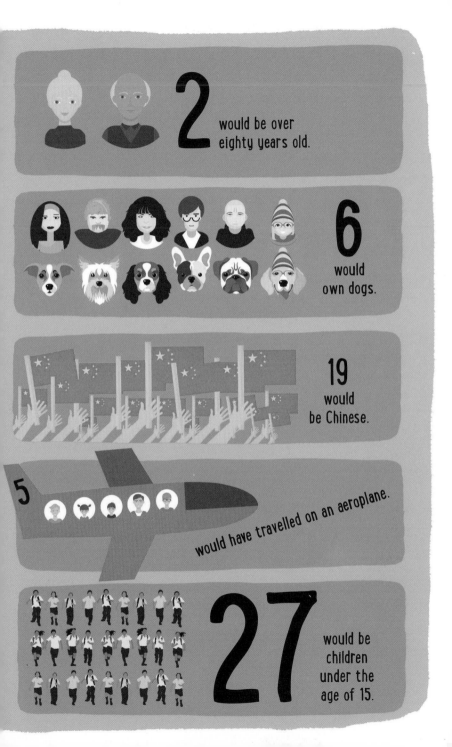

2 would be over eighty years old.

6 would own dogs.

19 would be Chinese.

5 would have travelled on an aeroplane.

27 would be children under the age of 15.

WHATEVER THE WEATHER

Some places don't really need a weather forecast.

Mount Wai'ale'ale, Hawaii, USA

Here it rains around 335 days of the year. Sometimes, one or two days a month are drier.

Atacama desert, Chile, South America

In some parts of the Atacama desert, it hasn't rained for more than 400 years.

The UK has a highly VARIABLE climate. It can be warm, cold, rainy, windy, snowy, misty, foggy... sometimes all on the same day!

Grand Banks, near Newfoundland, eastern Canada

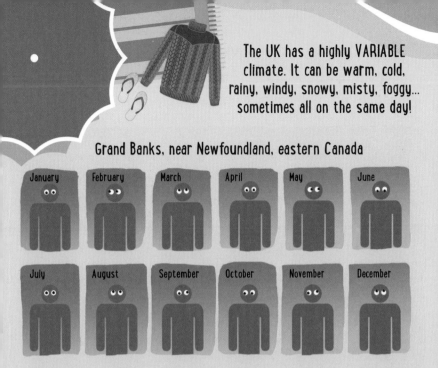

Beacause of the meeting of the Labrador Current and the Gulf Stream, fog forms pretty much every day.

Cape Denison, Antarctica

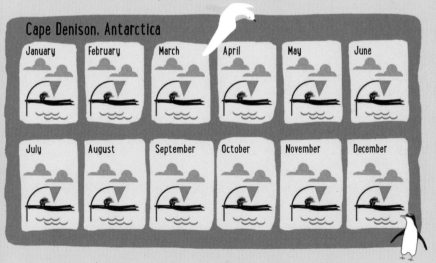

The windiest place on Earth: average wind speeds are 50km/h, but sometimes they can reach 200km/h.

TOILET TROUBLE

Going to the toilet is (usually) simple enough. But some people have had BIG trouble in the smallest room.

Most people have a poo once a day (on average).

24 hours

The world record for constipation (not being able to do a poo) is 45 days. Crikey. That's bunged up!

45 days

HOW LONG ARE YOU GONNA BE IN THERE?!

JANUARY

MARCH

APRIL

Most people take (on average) 21 seconds to have a wee.

21 seconds

But the world record for the longest wee is (apparently)...

8 minutes, 28 seconds

WELL, BLOW ME DOWN

The Beaufort scale is used to measure wind speed. It's measured by 'observed conditions'. So – how many of these conditions have YOU observed?

BEAUFORT SCALE 0

Less than 1km/h:
Smoke rises vertically.

BEAUFORT SCALE 1

1.1 to 5.5km/h:
Smoke drifts.

BEAUFORT SCALE 2

5.6 to 11km/h:
Leaves rustle in the trees.

BEAUFORT SCALE 4

20 to 28km/h:
Loose paper gets blown around.

BEAUFORT SCALE 6

39 to 49km/h:
Umbrellas become difficult to use.

BEAUFORT SCALE 8

62 to 74km/h:
Cars veer on the roads.

BEAUFORT SCALE 10

89 to 102km/h:
Trees are uprooted from the ground.

BEAUFORT SCALE 12

Greater than 118km/h:
Unsecured objects are hurled about.

The fastest wind speed ever measured was 408km/h, recorded during a hurricane on Barrow Island, Australia.

SORT IT OUT!

These letters need to be sorted into four postal sacks – for England, Scotland, Wales and the rest of the world. How quickly could you do this?

MR I. M. SKINT
1 ECONOMY DRIVE
LONDON IO5 P2U

MS IONA KATT
5 SOFT MEWS
CARDIFF MIO OWW

MR S. CAPE
5 RUNNER WAY
GLASGOW B1E B1E

MS MONA LOTT
10 KOMP LANE
MANCHESTER WH1 N1E

MR MILES AWAY
20 NOTVERRY CLOSE
AUSTRALIA UR2 FAA

Mr. S. Claus
Lapland
HOH OHO

WALES

SCOTLAND

ENGLAND

REST OF
THE WORLD

MR CLIFF TOPP
5 NEERTHER EDGE
DOVER KENT
UR2 H11
55p

MR RICH MANN
& MS MILLY O'NAIRE
1 BIGPAY RISE
NEW YORK,
NEW YORK
AIR MAIL
PAR AVION

MS O. LIMPIC
1 FURST PLACE
ATHENS,
GREECE

MR ED T. CHERR
55 TOTAL SQUARE
NORWICH D10 SHN

MR MIKE
ROWE-CHIPP
2 ILEKT ROAD
SAN FRANCISCO
01-01-01
FRAGILE

MR GENE YUSS
BRIGHT'S PARK
LONDON E99 HED

TOP
SECRET
MR CLARK KENT
6 SUPERHEAR ROW
SMALLVILLE
KANSAS, USA
PAR AVION

MR D. CREPPID
99 OVATHER HILL
OLDCASTLE,
IRELAND

Now – how long do
you think it would
take a sorting machine
to do the same job?

1 SECOND

That's right. The IRV 3000 sorting machine can correctly sort 14 letters in a second, even if the handwriting on the front of them is TERRIBLE.

And take a look at what these other incredible machines can do in one second...

Tianhe-2, a Chinese supercomputer, can make 33,860 trillion calculations.

NASA's New Horizons probe can travel 16 kilometres through space.

A camera created by the MIT Media Lab, in the USA, can take 1,000,000,000,000 (a trillion) pictures. It can even capture a photograph of light itself.

The Large Hadron Collider, in Switzerland, can shoot a beam of protons around a 27-kilometre tunnel 11,245 times.

THERE'S ALWAYS ONE

Some things in nature insist on being different.

The fish that climbs trees
The Indian climbing perch can breathe oxygen and pushes itself along with its fins and tail.

The flying snake
The golden tree snake pushes out its ribs and turns its whole body into a giant 'wing' for gliding through the air.

The frog with claws
The African clawed frog uses the claws on its hind feet to pull apart its food.

The poisonous bird
Touching a hooded pitohui's feathers causes numbness and tingling.

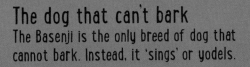

The dog that can't bark
The Basenji is the only breed of dog that cannot bark. Instead, it 'sings' or yodels.

DEEP TROUBLE

The Cave of the Swallows in Mexico, North America,
is the deepest cave shaft in the world.

The cave is popular
with base jumpers.

A hot air balloon once
floated down through the
cave's 49-metre opening and
landed safely on the floor

370
meters

If you jumped
without a parachute,
it would take you
about 10 seconds
to hit the bottom.

The cave is almost
four times the height
of London's Big Ben.

The floor of the cave is
covered with bird and bat
poo, snakes and scorpions.

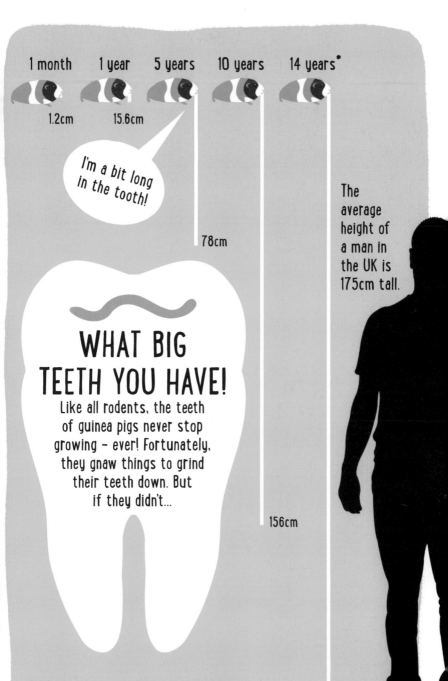

TOP TRUNKS

Elephants use their trunks for almost everything – and would not survive without them. This family album shows just some of the ways in which they use their nifty noses.

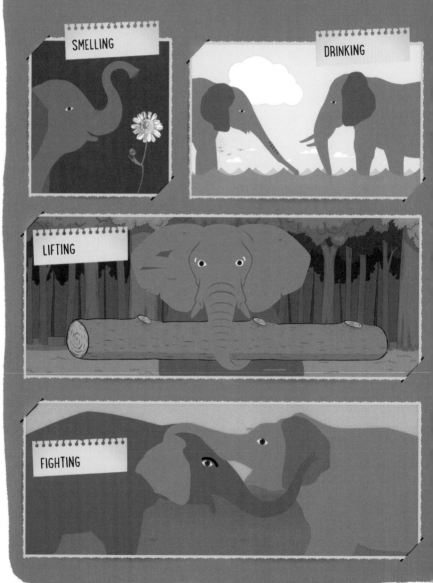

SMELLING

DRINKING

LIFTING

FIGHTING

BEYOND BELIEF

Black cats. Friday the 13th. Lucky horseshoes. British people have some funny superstitions – but what about other countries?

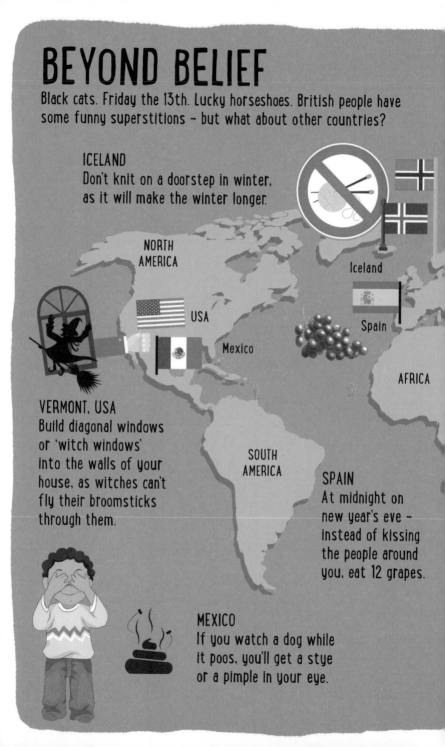

ICELAND
Don't knit on a doorstep in winter, as it will make the winter longer.

NORTH AMERICA

Iceland

USA

Spain

Mexico

AFRICA

VERMONT, USA
Build diagonal windows or 'witch windows' into the walls of your house, as witches can't fly their broomsticks through them.

SOUTH AMERICA

SPAIN
At midnight on new year's eve – instead of kissing the people around you, eat 12 grapes.

MEXICO
If you watch a dog while it poos, you'll get a stye or a pimple in your eye.

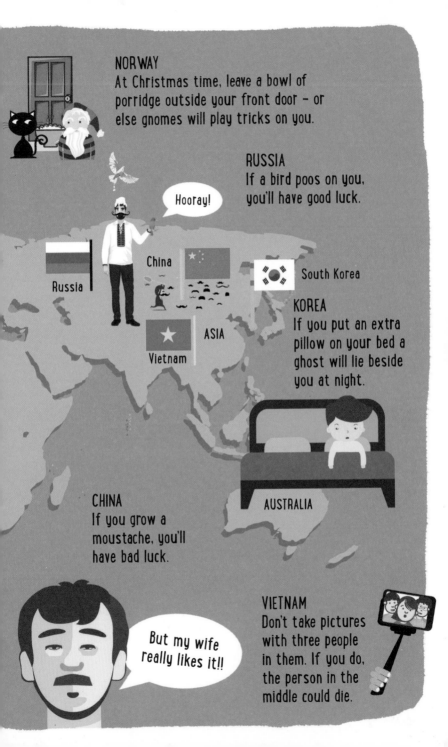

Purr-fectly understandable

A cat's "miaow" sounds the same to almost everyone: "miaou" (French), "miau" (German and Italian), "miyau" (Russian).

HARD TO SWALLOW

We eat a lot of food on purpose. But what about the other stuff we swallow, which maybe we don't like to think about?

The average person swallows 1kg of insects each year.

That's the same weight as seven apples.

You also swallow about 365 litres of snot a year.

That's enough to fill two oil barrels.

And about 500 litres of saliva.

That's enough to fill a large wheelie bin or dumpster.

As well as all that – in one year, the average person also inhales (breathes in):

Dozens of grams of their own dead skin.

Dozens of grams of human and animal hair.

Thousands of dust mite droppings, dust mite eggs and dead dust mites.

Thousands of grains of pollen.

Millions of spores (flying particles) of fungus and mould.

Unless you are allergic to any of these things, this is all COMPLETELY NORMAL – so,
ENJOY YOUR MEAL!

A SQUASH
AND A SQUEEZE

Most animals can fit through a hole as long as it's bigger than their head. But some animals are even squashier than that.

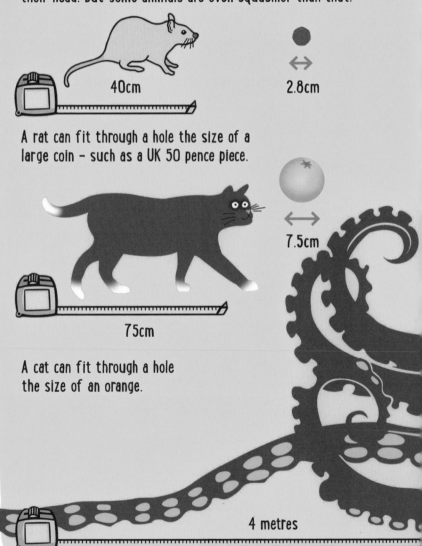

40cm

2.8cm

A rat can fit through a hole the size of a large coin – such as a UK 50 pence piece.

7.5cm

75cm

A cat can fit through a hole the size of an orange.

4 metres

But the King of Squashiness is the Pacific octopus. This huge beast has a four-metre arm span – and yet it can fit through a hole the size of a tennis ball!

6.5cm

20CM

15CM

HERE WE GROW
How long would it take each of these plants to grow as high as this page (20 centimetres)?

10CM

5CM

BAMBOO	PACIFIC KELP	JAPANESE ARROWROOT
5 HOURS	**8 HOURS**	**16 HOURS**

IT BITES!

The Schmidt pain index measures the most painful insect bites and stings known to humankind. So, who are the creepy culprits to watch out for?

Pain index 0

LADYBIRD
They can bite, but they barely even break the skin – so if you're nipped by one you'll rarely feel it.

Pain index 1

SWEAT BEE
So called because they are attracted to the tasty salt in your sweat. Their sting is like a 'tiny spark'.

OW...

EH?

Turn over for the
King of the Stingers.

Pain index 2

BALD-FACED HORNET
Females defend their nest
by stinging again and again.
The stings hurt for
about 24 hours.

OUCH!

Pain index 3

RED HARVESTER ANT
As well as injecting highly
painful venom with their
stingers, these ants also
deliver a nasty bite
from their jaws.

ARGH!

ZAP!!
POW!!

Pain index 4+

BULLET ANT
Given this name because its sting is like being shot. This is the most painful insect sting in the world by far.

AIEEE!!!

Pain index 4

TARANTULA HAWK
This wasp is HUGE – five centimetres long – and hunts tarantulas. Its sting has been compared to electrocution.

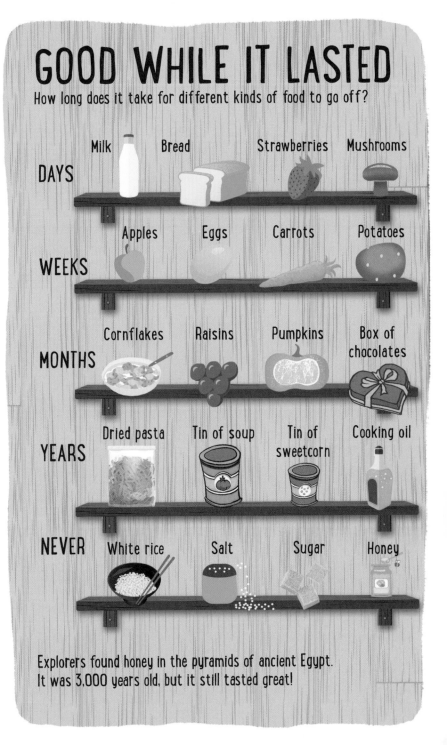

BABY TALK

The simple fact of having a baby can
land a lady in the record books...

2 Average number of babies
per woman*:

(*Rounded down from the exact average figure of 2.33.)

The most babies born to a single woman:

69 This is the number of babies born to the wife
of Feodor Vassilyev in 18th-century Russia.

This is the average weight
of a newborn baby.

3.34kg

Italy, 1955: the heaviest
baby ever born to a
healthy mother.

10.65kg

This is like giving birth to a
one-and-a-half-year-old toddler!

One in 30 babies is born with a twin brother or sister.

One-third of twins are identical.

One in 2,000 babies is born with teeth.

One in three babies born this year will live to be 100 or more.

SEASONS IN SPACE

In most places on Earth, each season lasts for about three months. But what about on other planets?

MERCURY:
NO REAL
SEASONS

EARTH:
3 MONTHS

JUPITER:
3 YEARS

VENUS:
55 DAYS

MARS:
6 MONTHS

SPINNING AROUND

The Earth's seasons are caused by the fact that its axis is slightly tilted. This means that different parts of the planet are closer to the Sun at different times of the year.

STORM DAMAGE

Whatever the season, it's best
to avoid Jupiter's Great Red Spot. This is
a gigantic, raging storm that's normally
between 18,000 and 24,000 kilometres wide (but slowly
getting smaller) where the winds blow at up to 680km/h.

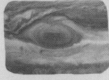

SATURN:
5 YEARS

URANUS:
20 YEARS

NEPTUNE:
40 YEARS

LET IT SNOW

Even during its 20-year-long summer,
Uranus's surface temperature rarely rises
above −200°C. The coldest temperature
ever recorded on Earth was −89.2°C
at Vostock Station, a Russian research
station in Antarctica.

GOOD EGG

An ostrich egg is the biggest egg in the world.
And guess what? It's edible!

A HARD-BOILED OSTRICH EGG

Feeds: 20 people
You will need:
1 x ostrich egg
1 x huge vat of boiling water
1 x garden wheelbarrow
1 x drill

METHOD

1. Take your wheelbarrow to a shop or farm that sells ostrich eggs. You'll need the wheelbarrow because an ostrich egg weighs in at around 2kg. That's the same as 40 chicken's eggs.

One of these...

...equals 40 of these:

Ostrich egg

Chicken eggs

2. Back in your kitchen, pour 30 litres of water into the large vat. That's about as much water as you'd use while taking a five-minute shower.

3. Plop your giant egg into the vat and boil it for 90 minutes. While you're waiting, you might want do something else that lasts for an hour-and-a-half. For example:

Fly the 645km from London to Edinburgh.

Watch 18 episodes of 'Pingu'.

Play in a football match (without a half-time break).

4. Break the shell of your hard-boiled egg using the drill. This is sensible because ostrich eggshells are 3mm thick – roughly the same thickness as a British pound coin. Even when they're not boiled, you can stand on an ostrich egg – and it won't break.

BOOM!

The loudest noise heard in modern history was created by the eruption of a volcano called Krakatoa in 1883.
So how loud are we talking?

Arctic
Ocean

NORTH
AMERICA

New York
City, USA

ACROSS THE PLANET

The pressure wave from the eruption registered on 'barographs' on the other side of the world for five days after the explosion.

Pacific
Ocean

Atlantic
Ocean

AFRICA

COLD SNAP

After the eruption, summer temperatures all around the world fell by 1.2°C – and it took five years for the climate to return to normal.

SOUTH
AMERICA

Southern
Ocean

BLUE MOON

The ash thrown up by the eruption made the sky dark all over the planet for years afterwards. It caused incredible red sunsets in several countries. People also said that the Moon sometimes looked blue – and sometimes green.

ASIA

NEARBY SEAS
Sailors on the sea close by suffered from burst eardrums.

Indian Ocean

PERTH, AUSTRALIA
People here heard the eruption – more than 3,110km away!

Southeast Asia

Krakatoa, Indonesia

AUSTRALIA

Perth

Rodrigues

RODRIGUES, INDIAN OCEAN
On this island, 4,800km away, people thought the noise was cannon fire from a passing ship.

KING OF THE FLINGERS

Food throwing festivals take place all over the world.
But which festive flingers throw the most?

BATTLE OF THE ORANGES, ITALY

500 TONNES

OF ORANGES

That's the same weight as:

3 BLUE WHALES

SPLAT!

Perhaps the most fun food-throwing party is the World Custard Pie Throwing Championships – held in Kent, England. You get maximum points if you manage to land a pie in someone's face.

Delicious!

LA TOMATINA, SPAIN

130 TONNES
OF TOMATOES

LA RAIMA, SPAIN

90 TONNES
OF GRAPES

That's the same weight as:

11 DOUBLE DECKER BUSES

That's the same weight as:

3 SHERMAN TANKS

SUPERBUGS

Some creepy crawlies are pretty darn tough. But there's one critter that can deal with almost ANY situation...

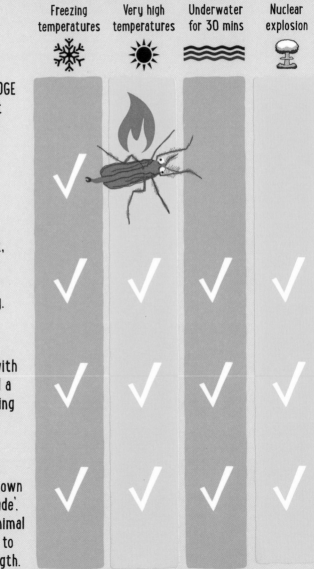

	Freezing temperatures ❄	Very high temperatures ☀	Underwater for 30 mins 〰	Nuclear explosion ☁
ANTARCTIC MIDGE A small insect that lives on the southern continent of Antarctica.	✓			
COCKROACH A large insect, with four wings, that eats anything.	✓	✓	✓	✓
SCORPION An arachnid with big claws and a dangerous sting in its tail.	✓	✓	✓	✓
WATER BEAR Technically known as a 'tardigrade', this micro-animal measures up to 0.5mm in length.	✓	✓	✓	✓

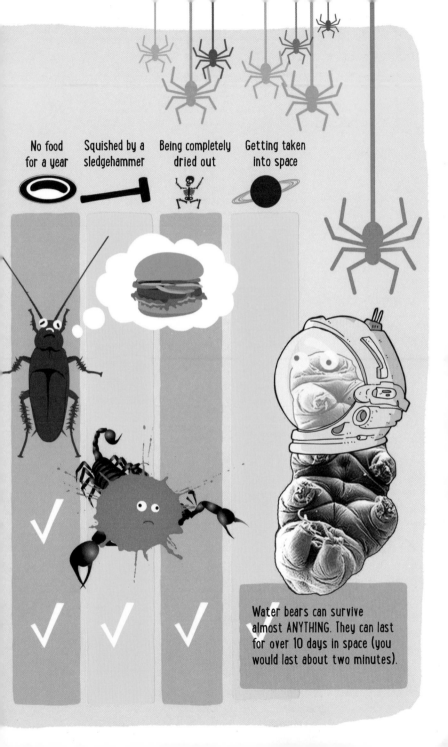

No food for a year

Squished by a sledgehammer

Being completely dried out

Getting taken into space

Water bears can survive almost ANYTHING. They can last for over 10 days in space (you would last about two minutes).

WHAT'S HOT

The hottest temperature ever created on Earth was 2 billion°C.
Just how hot IS that?

2 BILLION°C

2 BILLION°C
The Z machine
(see below), USA, 2006.

150 MILLION°C
A nuclear fusion reactor.

30,000°C
A bolt of lightning.

1 BILLION°C
The core of a
red giant (a huge,
expanding star).

15 MILLION°C
The Sun's core
(central region).

THE Z MACHINE
Officially known as the 'Z Pulsed Power Facility',
this is the largest X-ray generator in the world.
It is located in New Mexico, in the USA.

TRUE COLOURS

Some things in nature are not the colour you'd expect.

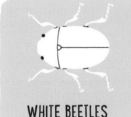

WHITE BEETLES

The tiny scales on the covering of a ghost beetle are possibly the whitest things in the natural world – even whiter than milk, or your teeth.

GREEN SAND

Papakolea beach in Hawaii, USA, gets its green colouring from olivine, a volcanic material that is plentiful in that area.

RED WATERFALL

Blood Falls, in Antarctica, flows out of a lake in a glacier. The lake has been turned bright red by the iron in the water.

BLUE LAVA

Kawah Ijen is a volcano in Indonesia. It spews out lava that is red by day and turquoise-blue by night. The change in colour is due to the high levels of sulphur in the hot, molten rock.

HELP!

There used to be a lot more animals in the world...

SUMATRAN ORANGUTANS
In 1900, there were...

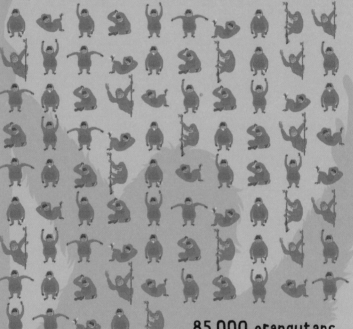

...85,000 orangutans.

TODAY...

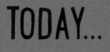

...just 6,000 orangutans.

KEY

=

1,000 orangutans

TIGERS
In 1900, there were...

...100,000 tigers.

TODAY...

...only 4,000 tigers.

KEY

=

1,000
tigers

BLUE WHALES
In 1900, there were...

...250,000 blue whales.

TODAY...

...there are about 5,000 blue whales.
The blue whale is the largest animal that has ever
existed on this planet. To find out more about protecting
Earth's endangered animals, visit www.worldwildlife.org

KEY

= 1,000 whales

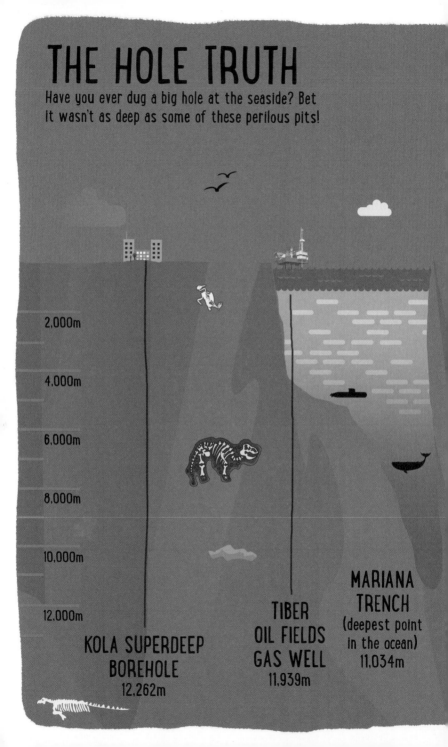

THE HOLE TRUTH

Have you ever dug a big hole at the seaside? Bet it wasn't as deep as some of these perilous pits!

2,000m

4,000m

6,000m

8,000m

10,000m

12,000m

KOLA SUPERDEEP BOREHOLE
12,262m

TIBER OIL FIELDS GAS WELL
11,939m

MARIANA TRENCH
(deepest point in the ocean)
11,034m

The very centre of the Earth's inner core lies 6,371,000 metres below the planet's surface.

TAUTONA MINE
(deepest mine in the world)
3,900m

THE VALLEY UNDER BYRD GLACIER
(deepest point on the Earth's surface)
2,780m

KRUBERA CAVE
(deepest cave in the world)
2,197m

SNOLAB
(deepest underground science lab)
2,100m

NOT BORING ANYMORE

The Kola Superdeep Borehole was drilled in an effort to get as deep as possible into the Earth's crust. The drilling was stopped in 1992, because the temperatures in the hole reached 180°C. This threatened to break the giant drill bits used to dig downwards. A new project – the 2012 MoHole To The Mantle – aims to go even deeper!

GUILTY CREATURES?

Can you arrest an animal? Looks like you can...

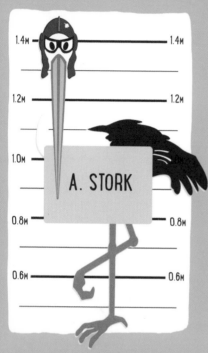

1.4M — 1.4M
1.2M — 1.2M
1.0M — 1.0M
0.8M — 0.8M
0.6M — 0.6M

A. STORK

1.0M — 1.0M
0.8M — 0.8M
0.6M — 0.6M
0.4M — 0.4M
0.2M — 0.2M

DR. G. OAT

In Egypt, in 2013, a stork was arrested for spying after a fisherman saw an electronic device on its back. It was actually a tagging device put there by scientists.

Police in Nigeria arrested a goat for armed robbery in January, 2009. They said the thief had used black magic to turn himself into a goat after trying to steal a car.

I saw him bury the bones, Your Honour.

DID YOU KNOW

that a dog is the only animal whose evidence can be used in a court of law?

I'm outta here.

1.4m — 1.4m

1.2m

1.0

0.6m

MR. DON KEY

— 1.0m

0.8m

0.6m — 0.6m

0.4m — 0.4m

MONK, E.Y.

In 2008, a donkey was arrested for assault in Mexico after it kicked two men. The animal was released when its owner agreed to pay the victims' medical bills.

A monkey got in trouble with the law in Pakistan, in 2008, for being an illegal immigrant. It had walked all the way from India. Eventually, the animal was given to a zoo in Pakistan.

EVIDENCE

from bloodhounds and police sniffer dogs can be used to pin criminals to crime scenes.

Good boy!

HOWDY, NEIGHBOUR!

It's not easy living on an island. Your nearest neighbours could be many kilometres away.

34KM

GT. BRITAIN   **FRANCE**

280KM

ICELAND   **GREENLAND**

500KM

MADAGASCAR   **MOZAMBIQUE**

1,700KM

NEW ZEALAND   **NEW CALEDONIA**

2,000KM

TRISTAN DE CUNHA   **SAINT HELENA**

Key to scale: 1 wave = 100km

North America
Europe
Atlantic Ocean
Asia
Africa
South America
Australia

Tristan de Cunha, in the southern Atlantic Ocean, is the most remote island in the world. Around 297 people live there, sharing just eight surnames.

ALL FINE IN THE END

The most overdue library book EVER was borrowed from Sidney Sussex College library, UK, in 1667 and returned 288 years later.

Universities charge about 10 pence per day for overdue books. So, if the college had imposed a fine, it would have been £10,519.20. That's enough money to buy...

...approximately 1,750 books – enough to create a new library!

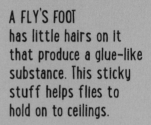

GECKOS
have tiny hairs on their feet, which create an electrostatic charge and act like magnets to stick them to a surface.

A FLY'S FOOT
has little hairs on it that produce a glue-like substance. This sticky stuff helps flies to hold on to ceilings.

SNAILS
produce a slimy mucus that helps them to cling on to anything and everything.

HANGING AROUND
Some animals can stick to the ceiling, while others can spend hours upside down. How do they do it?

BATS
hang on to
branches or cave
walls using their
special talons. This
means they can
take off quickly
by just letting go.

BABY POSSUMS
are so light that they
can hang on to branches
with their tails. This
way, they can keep all
four hands free!

A MANATEE
doesn't hang upside down, but it's
one of the few sea creatures that
loves to sleep upside down – ideally
on a nice, comfy sandbank.

**A SPIDER MONKEY'S
'PREHENSILE' TAIL**
can grow up to 90cm
long and is used as
a fifth hand.

STRANGE BUT TRUE

Some countries have some very strange rules.

In Capri, Italy, it is against the law to wear 'noisy footwear'.

In the UK, it is an act of treason to place a postage stamp upside down, if it bears the image of the British monarch (king or queen).

In Germany, it is illegal to run out of petrol on the motorway.

In Florida, USA, it is unlawful for an unmarried woman to do a parachute jump on a Sunday.

In Arizona, USA, it is against the law to keep a donkey in a bathtub.

In Thailand, it is illegal to step on a banknote.

In Eraclea, Italy, it is against the law to build a sandcastle.

In Salt Lake City, USA, it is illegal to walk down the street carrying a violin in a paper bag.

In Wilbur, Washington, USA, it is against the law to ride an ugly horse.

GET OFF MY LAND!

Animals often have a lot of territory to defend.
How do they manage it..?

First of all, they 'mark' it by...

SPRAYING
In other words, weeing.
Cats and dogs are examples
of animals that do this.

SCENT MARKING
Some animals have special
scent glands that they rub
against the edges of their
burrow or territory.

VISUAL SIGN-POSTS
The lynx and black bear chew
and scratch trees, leaving
behind tufts of fur as
'territorial markers'.

Then they have to **FIGHT** to defend it.

But how much territory are we talking about..?

A FOOTBALL FIELD = 1.5 ACRES

SQUIRREL: 15 ACRES

URBAN FOX: 50 ACRES

BADGER: 120 ACRES

BALD EAGLE: 1,000 ACRES

RHINO: 2,000 ACRES

THERE'S THAT FOOTBALL
PITCH AGAIN (1.5 ACRES).

TIGER:
20,000 ACRES

Welcome to
my pad!

A SIBERIAN TIGER
has an even bigger range than
this. Typically, its territory
covers about 128,000 acres,
which is more than 500 square
kilometres of land. Using the
same scale as this page, we'd
need TEN MORE PAGES to show
this animal's territory.

THE STORY OF THE SUN

To cut a VERY long story short...

4.75 billion years ago

A star exploded and sent off a huge shock wave. (This is called a supernova.)

Not too far away, a large cloud of gas and dust was minding its own business.

The shock wave from the supernova caused some of the gas and dust to squash together.

As this gas and dust fused together it created lots of heat and light.

A star was born.

Some of the gas and dust kept floating around the star.

EARTH

THE SUN

These materials would later become the planets.

Today

The Sun is halfway through its life. It is already 30 per cent more luminous (bright and shining) than when it was first formed.

In 5.6 billion years' time

The Sun will have burnt up all of its hydrogen – and it will start to grow much bigger.

In 7.1 billion years' time

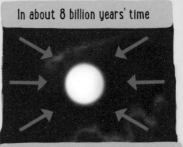

The Sun will become a 'red giant'. It will swallow up Mercury, Venus, Earth – and probably Mars, too.

But on the plus side...

Saturn's largest moon, Titan (currently a chilly -179°C), may be warm enough to support life.

In about 8 billion years' time

The Sun will start to shrink and turn into a 'white dwarf' – a very dense, planet-sized object.

In a quadrillion years' time

THE SUN

The Sun will be a tiny, icy-cold object (about -270°C) sitting in the chilly blackness of space.

In 10 quintillion years' time

THE SUN

The Sun's remains will eventually get pulled into the supermassive black hole at the centre of our galaxy, the Milky Way.

...THEN IT'LL START ALL OVER AGAIN. AND AGAIN. AND AGAIN...

A MOOSE IN THE HOOSE

Towser the cat caught a record 28,899 mice over the course of his life in a whisky distillery in Scotland, UK. That's an average of:

3 MICE A DAY

24 MICE A WEEK

100 MICE A MONTH

PURR-FECT
WHISKY

When Towser died, the distillery got another cat,
called Amber. It did not catch a single mouse.

BOLT FROM THE BLUE

Lightning is one of the most powerful forces on Earth. Here are some 'striking' things that you should know about it...

THERE'S A LOT OF IT
There are around 100 lightning strikes happening somewhere in the Earth's atmosphere...

...EVERY SECOND!

BUT MOST OF IT DOESN'T HIT THE GROUND.
80 per cent of lightning happens inside clouds or travels from one cloud to another.

20%

Ha-HA. Missed!

LIGHTNING BOLTS CONTAIN LOTS OF ENERGY
Five billion joules of energy, in fact. That's enough energy to...

Make 100,000 slices of toast.

Drive the average car 1,500km.

LIGHTNING CAN STRIKE YOU IN DIFFERENT WAYS

DIRECT
The least common way is when it hits your body directly.

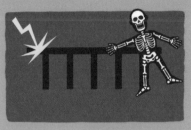

CONTACT
When it hits something you're holding that conducts electricity.

SPLASH
This is when lightning jumps from a nearby object to a person.

BLAST
The lightning hits an object and causes a shockwave.

BUT YOUR CHANCES OF BEING HIT BY LIGHTNING ARE VERY, VERY LOW.
If you take 10 million people, this is how they are most likely to die:

- 4 million: from a heart attack or stroke.
- 1,500: road accidents.
- 20: train accidents.
- 15: drowning in the bath.
- 5: falling out of bed.
- 5: falling off a ladder.
- 3: venomous snake bites.
- 3: food poisoning.

Just 1 will die from being struck by lightning.

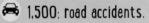

DISASTER!

The Earth has already faced five global, mass extinctions – but what happened, exactly?

1. END-ORDOVICIAN MASS EXTINCTION, 445–440 MILLION YEARS AGO

WHAT EXISTED: Nearly all animals lived in the sea.

Nautiloids

Trilobites

Conodonts

Brachiopods

Echinoderms

WHAT HAPPENED: A massive ice age. Sea levels fell and then rose.

WHAT DIED OUT: Roughly 9 out of 10 of ALL species.

| 500 MILLION YEARS AGO | 400 MILLION YEARS AGO | 300 MILLION YEARS AGO |

▲ ▲ ▲

2. LATE DEVONIAN MASS EXTINCTION, 375–359 MILLION YEARS AGO

WHAT EXISTED: Lots of fish. Some insects and the ancestors (early relatives) of amphibians.

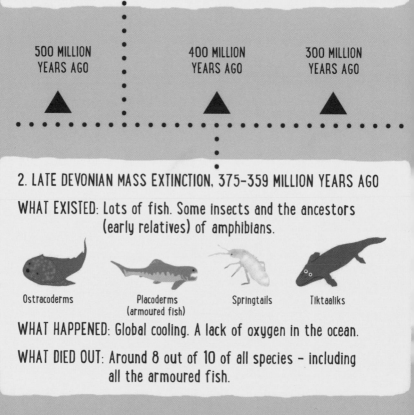

Ostracoderms

Placoderms (armoured fish)

Springtails

Tiktaaliks

WHAT HAPPENED: Global cooling. A lack of oxygen in the ocean.

WHAT DIED OUT: Around 8 out of 10 of all species – including all the armoured fish.

3. END-PERMIAN MASS EXTINCTION, 252–248 MILLION YEARS AGO

WHAT EXISTED: Fish, insects, amphibians and the first reptiles.

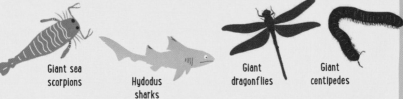

Giant sea scorpions

Hydodus sharks

Giant dragonflies

Giant centipedes

WHAT HAPPENED: Very high temperatures. A huge volcanic explosion.

WHAT DIED OUT: Almost all species. Around 4 per cent survived.

200 MILLION YEARS AGO

100 MILLION YEARS AGO

4. END-TRIASSIC MASS EXTINCTION, 201–200 MILLION YEARS AGO

WHAT EXISTED: Lots of sea and land creatures, including the very first dinosaurs.

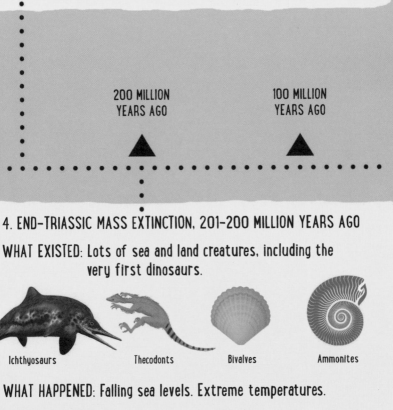

Ichthyosaurs

Thecodonts

Bivalves

Ammonites

WHAT HAPPENED: Falling sea levels. Extreme temperatures.

WHAT DIED OUT: About 80 per cent of all species.

5. END-CRETACEOUS MASS EXTINCTION, 66-65 MILLION YEARS AGO

WHAT EXISTED: Dinosaurs, pterosaurs and more.

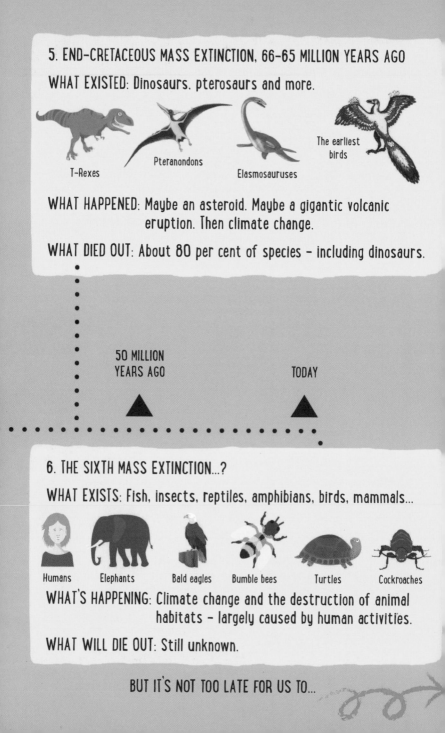

T-Rexes

Pteranondons

Elasmosauruses

The earliest birds

WHAT HAPPENED: Maybe an asteroid. Maybe a gigantic volcanic eruption. Then climate change.

WHAT DIED OUT: About 80 per cent of species – including dinosaurs.

50 MILLION YEARS AGO

TODAY

6. THE SIXTH MASS EXTINCTION...?

WHAT EXISTS: Fish, insects, reptiles, amphibians, birds, mammals...

Humans   Elephants   Bald eagles   Bumble bees   Turtles   Cockroaches

WHAT'S HAPPENING: Climate change and the destruction of animal habitats – largely caused by human activities.

WHAT WILL DIE OUT: Still unknown.

BUT IT'S NOT TOO LATE FOR US TO...

...SAVE THE WORLD!

By making small changes, we can make a BIG difference.

THINGS THAT MAKE A **BIG** DIFFERENCE

Use energy-saving light bulbs.

Fill the kettle ONLY with the amount of water you need.

Avoid 'standby'. Turn devices off – completely – when you're not using them.

THINGS THAT MAKE A **VERY BIG** DIFFERENCE

Only switch the heating on when you really need it.

Hang your clothes out rather than using a tumble dryer.

Walk and cycle whenever you can, instead of going by car.

THINGS THAT MAKE AN **ENORMOUS** DIFFERENCE

Get insulation for your loft. Stops rising heat from escaping.

Make your own energy – put solar panels on the roof!

Try not to fly. Planes are cool – but they use lots of fuel!

ANIMAL LOVERS
What are the most popular pets in the United Kingdom?

300,000
snakes

200,000
newts and salamanders

8.5 MILLION

DOGS

1 million
rabbits

1 million
caged birds

500,000
hamsters

500,000
guinea pigs

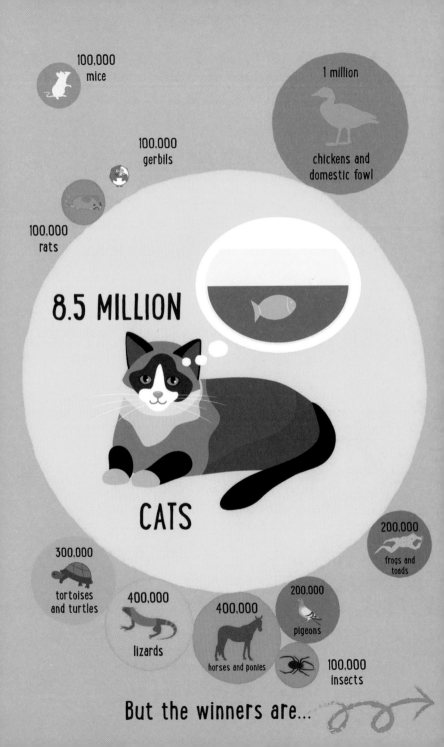

50 MILLION

FISH

(ABOUT 25 MILLION IN TANKS)

(ROUGHLY 25 MILLION
IN GARDEN PONDS)

FEED ME!

Little animals can have big appetites.

The pygmy shrew weighs four grams, but has to eat FIVE grams of food a day. That's 25 per cent more than its own bodyweight.

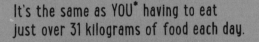

4g

5g

It's the same as YOU* having to eat just over 31 kilograms of food each day.

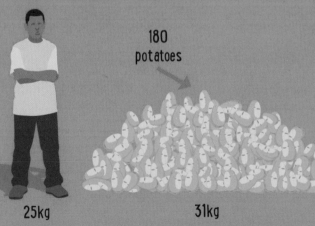

180 potatoes

25kg

31kg

31kg is also the same as eating 500 carrots or 24 whole chickens EVERY SINGLE DAY.

*(The average eight-year-old weighs around 25kg.)

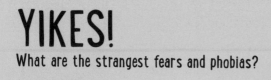

YIKES!
What are the strangest fears and phobias?

Boo!

FRANCOPHOBIA
Fear of French people.

OMPHALOPHOBIA
A fear of belly buttons.

DIDASKALEINOPHOBIA
Fear of school

TUROPHOBIA
Fear of cheese.

ABLUTOPHOBIA
The fear of having a bath.

PELADOPHOBIA
A fear
of bald
people.

"13"

TRISKAIDEKAPHOBIA
Fear of the number 13.

AULOPHOBIA
Fear of flutes.

GENUPHOBIA
Fear of knees.

XANTHOPHOBIA
The fear of the
colour yellow.

PANPHOBIA
The fear of
EVERYTHING.

I'M A SURVIVOR
How to escape a deadly animal attack!

CROCODILE

1. RUN. A human's top speed is faster than a crocodile's.

2. If it catches you, FIGHT. It prefers an easy meal.

DEFINITELY DON'T
run in a zigzag. You'll trip over and the croc will be able to see you more easily.

TIGER

1. Hide in a place where the tiger can't see you.

2. If there's nowhere to hide, scream and BE FIERCE.

DEFINITELY DON'T
Play dead. Tigers won't be fooled and they just LOVE animals that can't fight back.

BEAR

1. Back away, SLOWLY.

Easy now, big fella!

2. If that doesn't work, stay still and wave your arms to make yourself look as big as possible.

DEFINITELY DON'T
Climb up into a tree. Most bears are very good climbers.

BULL

What are YOU looking at?!

1. Jump over the nearest fence.

2. If there's no fence, sidestep the bull and RUN in the opposite direction.

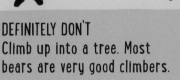

DEFINITELY DON'T
run in the SAME direction as the bull. That's one race you'll definitely lose.

AND HERE'S THE BEST ADVICE OF ALL: DON'T GO NEAR THESE ANIMALS IN THE FIRST PLACE. THEY'RE REALLY DANGEROUS.

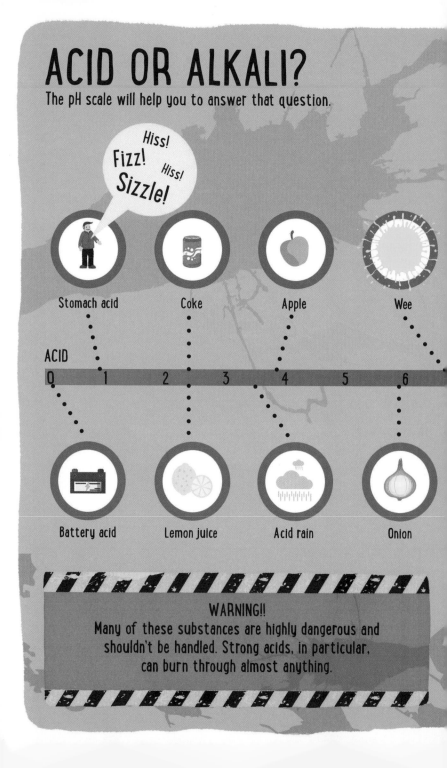

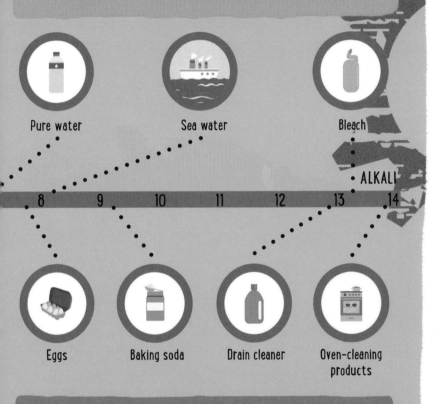

THE ACID TEST
Your stomach acid is very strong. It can dissolve almost anything – including bones, cloth and some metals. 'Gastric mucus', produced by the lining of the stomach, stops the acid from harming your insides.

Pure water

Sea water

Bleach

ALKALI

8 9 10 11 12 13 14

Eggs

Baking soda

Drain cleaner

Oven-cleaning products

ELBOW GREASE
Alkalis are found in lots of cleaning products. They absorb greasy and oily substances – and prevent them from being smeared back all over the surface you're trying to clean.

IT TAKES SOME BEATING

The hearts of different animals beat at different rates.

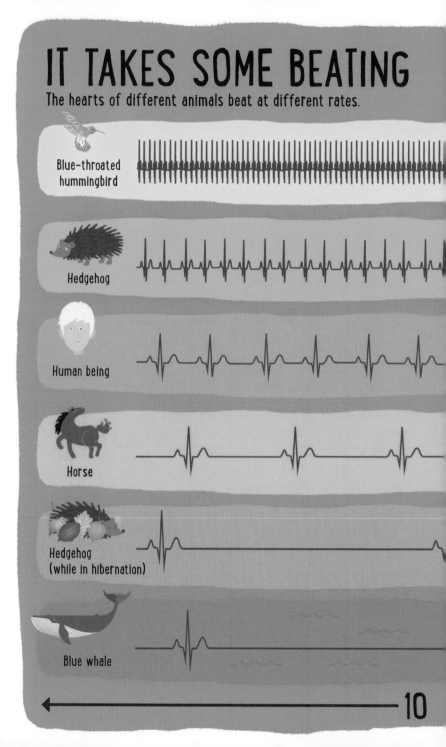

Blue-throated
hummingbird

Hedgehog

Human being

Horse

Hedgehog
(while in hibernation)

Blue whale

10

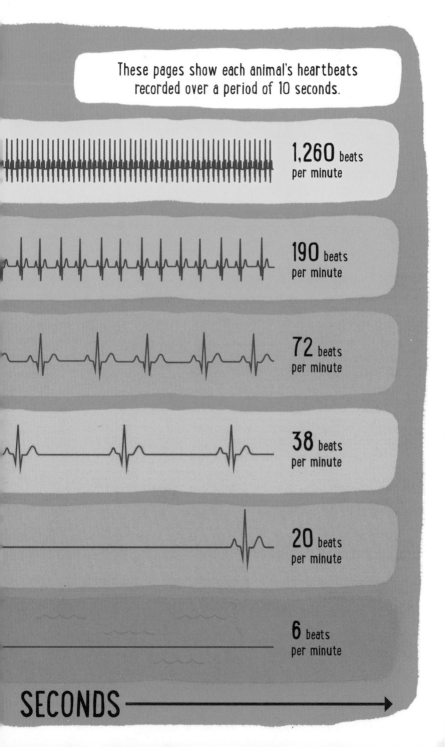

These pages show each animal's heartbeats recorded over a period of 10 seconds.

1,260 beats per minute

190 beats per minute

72 beats per minute

38 beats per minute

20 beats per minute

6 beats per minute

SECONDS

I CAN SEE A RAINBOW

What's the world's favourite colour?

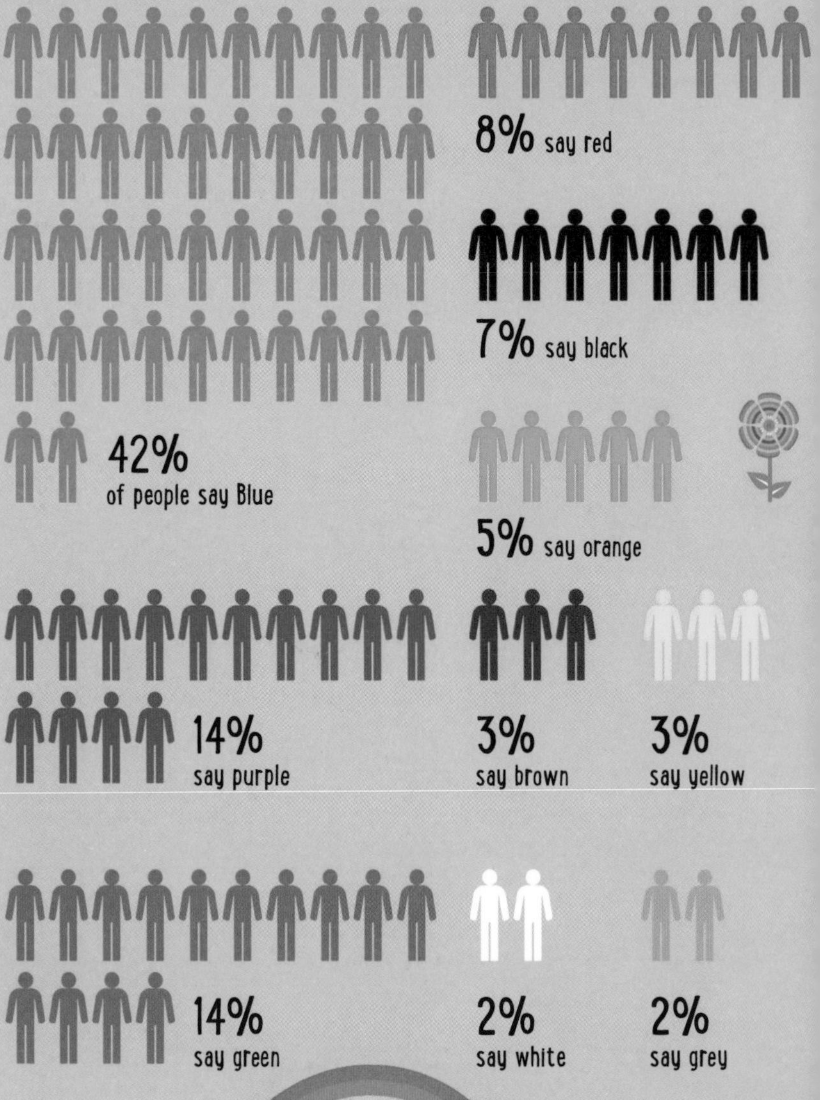

8% say red

7% say black

5% say orange

42%
of people say Blue

14%
say purple

3%
say brown

3%
say yellow

14%
say green

2%
say white

2%
say grey

Some people believe that you can tell a lot about people by their favourite colour. What's YOUR favourite colour? Do you agree with the descriptions below?

Blue? You're quiet and calm, thoughtful and hard-working.

Red? You are outgoing and athletic. You like to live life to the full.

Green? Green people are sensible and balanced, with lots of friends.

Orange? You're happy and good-natured. You don't get stressed too easily and you don't take life too seriously.

Brown? These people are steady and down-to-earth. They like to keep themselves to themselves.

Purple? You are sensitive and creative. You love arts and crafts.

Pink? You're affectionate and gentle. You are naturally kind, and don't like upsetting people.

Yellow? Yellow lovers are cheerful and hopeful. They always look on the bright, sunny side of life.

KAPOW!!

Animals like a bust-up. But what
are the most EPIC animal battles,
and which beast normally wins?

SCORPION
V
MEERKAT

SCORPION
Length: 14cm
Weight: 25g
Special powers: sharp claws and
a venomous stinger.

MEERKAT:
Length: 50cm (including tail)
Weight: 700g
Special powers: speed and super-sharp teeth.

WINNER: THE MEERKAT
A meerkat strikes fast, grabbing the scorpion and
biting off its nasty stinger.

COLOSSAL SQUID
V
SPERM WHALE

COLOSSAL SQUID:
Length: 12-14m
Weight: up to 0.5 tonnes
Walloping weapons: sharp, swivelling hooks on their arms.

SPERM WHALE:
Length: 15-18m
Weight: up to 40 tonnes
Walloping weapons: strong teeth and a head shaped
like a battering ram.

WINNER: THE SPERM WHALE
A large number of squid beaks have been found in the
stomachs of sperm whales. This suggests the whales
normally triumph – but not without a serious fight.

LION
V
GIRAFFE

AFRICAN LION:
Length: up to 2m
Weight: 120-190kg
Super powers: huge jaws and powerful muscles.

GIRAFFE:
Height: 4-6m
Weight: 0.8-1.2 tonnes
Super powers: a strong kick and hard hooves.

WINNER: THE GIRAFFE
One kick from a giraffe is fatal to a lion. For this reason,
lions usually attack only young or sick giraffes.

MONGOOSE
V
KING COBRA

MONGOOSE:
Length: up to 120cm (including tail)
Weight: up to 1.7kg
Battle abilities: quick reflexes and a powerful bite.

KING COBRA:
Length: up to 5.5m
Weight: up to 9kg
Battle abilities: can deliver enough venom, in
                 a single bite, to kill 20 people.

WINNER: THE MONGOOSE
The mongoose is easily fast enough to dodge the snake's
feisty bite. It is also immune to the venom, if it is bitten.
Its powerful jaws can kill the snake in one vicious SNAP!

MONSIEUR MANGETOUT

Michel Lotito, otherwise known as Monsieur Mangetout ('Mr Eats Everything'), was a French entertainer. He was known for his ability to eat VERY strange objects. Here are some of the strangest.

1

Cessna
light aircraft
(It took Lotito two years
to eat the whole thing.)

15 shopping trolleys

18 bicycles

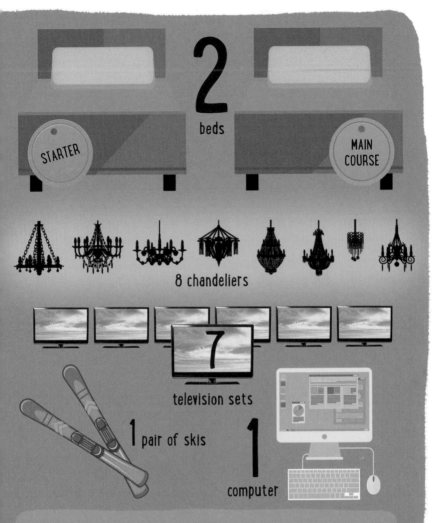

2 beds

STARTER

MAIN COURSE

8 chandeliers

7 television sets

1 pair of skis

1 computer

HOW DID HE DO IT?
His technique was to break the metal (and other materials) into small pieces, and then drink mineral oil to help him swallow them.

This diet would probably KILL anyone else, but Michel claimed that it didn't give him indigestion, and that it didn't hurt when he went for a poo!

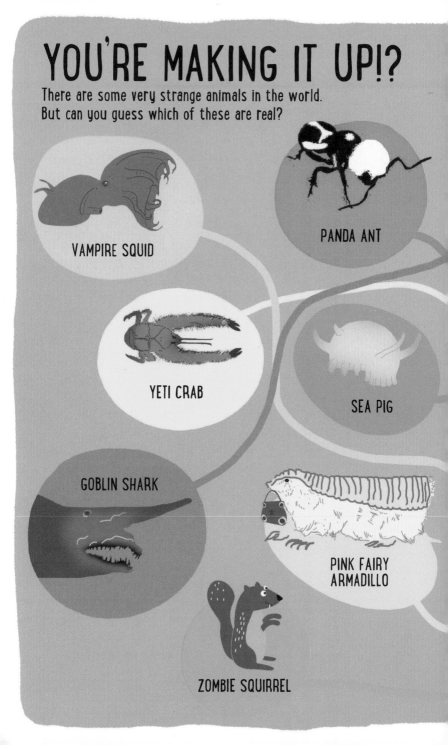

YOU'RE MAKING IT UP!?

There are some very strange animals in the world.
But can you guess which of these are real?

VAMPIRE SQUID

PANDA ANT

YETI CRAB

SEA PIG

GOBLIN SHARK

PINK FAIRY
ARMADILLO

ZOMBIE SQUIRREL

REAL
This slow-moving sneak can thrust its jaws forwards to snap up nearby fish.

NOT REAL
Dead squirrels tend not to rise from the grave and eat people's brains. PHEW!

REAL
With large, tube-like feet, these are the only species of sea cucumber that can walk around.

REAL
These furry-armed critters live near to deep, hot vents in the southern Pacific ocean.

REAL
This is actually a wasp that looks like a large, hairy ant. Because of its painful sting, it is known as 'the cow killer'.

REAL
This beast gets its name from its red eyes, spiny arms and cape-like webbing. (It doesn't actually drink blood.)

REAL
Its shell protects it from predators and its fur keeps it warm on the plains of Argentina.

BIG
DIFFERENCES
Evolution can make the same kinds of
animals gigantic or tiny. Take a look...

BIRDS
Largest bird

Smallest
bird

Ostrich:
2.5m tall

Bee hummingbird:
5.7cm long

REPTILES
Largest reptile

Saltwater crocodile:
5m long

Smallest
reptile

2p
coin

Dwarf
gecko:
18mm long

MAMMALS

Blue whale:
25-32m in length

Largest mammal
(and also the largest
creature ever to have
lived on planet Earth)

Bumbleebee bat:
3.3cm long

Etruscan shrew:
5.8cm long

THE SMALLEST MAMMALS
Although the bumbleebee bat
is shorter, the Etruscan shrew
is lighter, so they both get
called 'the smallest mammal'.

THAT'S A BIT RICH!

If someone gave you 1p and said they'd double it every day – how long would it take to become a millionaire? Six months? A year? Never..?

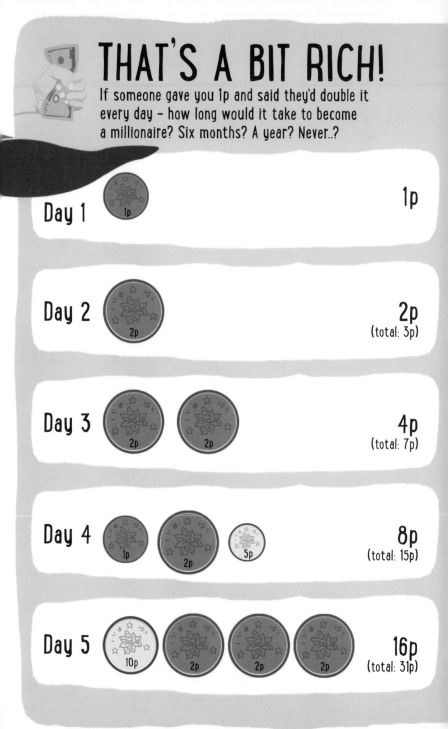

Day 1 — 1p

Day 2 — 2p
(total: 3p)

Day 3 — 4p
(total: 7p)

Day 4 — 8p
(total: 15p)

Day 5 — 16p
(total: 31p)

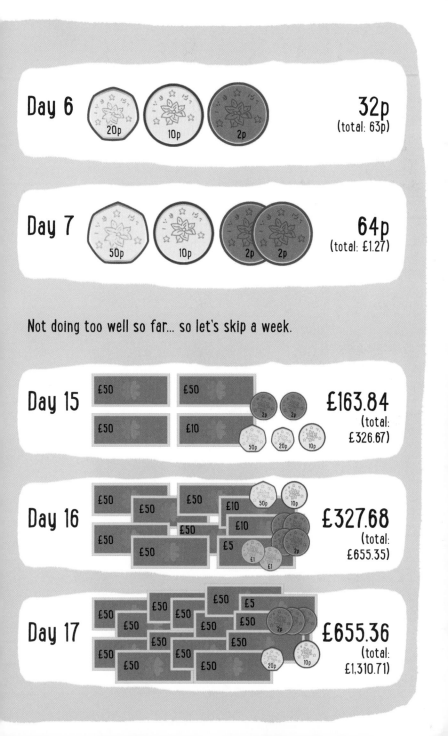

Day 6 20p 10p 2p **32p** (total: 63p)

Day 7 50p 10p 2p 2p **64p** (total: £1.27)

Not doing too well so far... so let's skip a week.

Day 15 £50 £50 £50 £10 2p 2p 50p 20p 10p **£163.84** (total: £326.67)

Day 16 £50 £50 £50 £10 50p 10p £50 £50 £10 £50 £5 £1 £1 2p **£327.68** (total: £655.35)

Day 17 £50 £50 £50 £50 £5 £50 £50 £50 £50 2p £50 £50 £50 £50 £50 £50 £50 £50 20p 10p **£655.36** (total: £1,310.71)

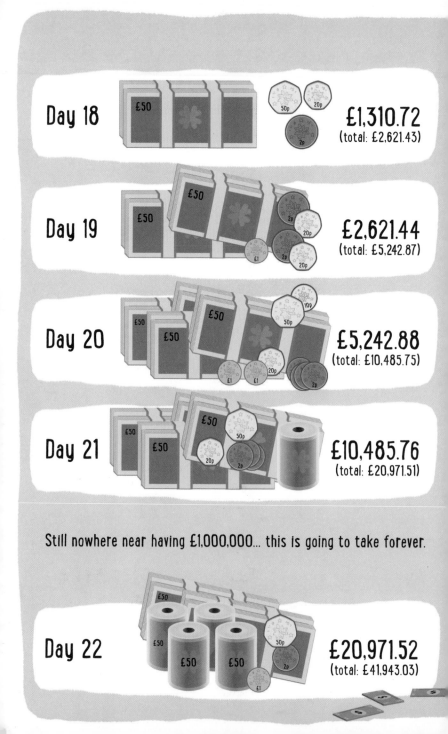

Day 18 — £1,310.72 (total: £2,621.43)

Day 19 — £2,621.44 (total: £5,242.87)

Day 20 — £5,242.88 (total: £10,485.75)

Day 21 — £10,485.76 (total: £20,971.51)

Still nowhere near having £1,000,000... this is going to take forever.

Day 22 — £20,971.52 (total: £41,943.03)

Day 23

£41,943.04
(total: £83,886.07)

Day 24
£83,886.08
(total: £167,772.15)

Day 25
£167,772.16
(total: £335,544.31)

Day 26
£335,544.32
(total: £671,088.63)

Day 27
£671,088.64
(total: £1,342,177.27)

SO, IN LESS THAN A MONTH, YOU'D BE A MILLIONAIRE.
Starting with just 1p...

SOURCES

This book would not have been possible without a wide range of other books, not to mention magazines, websites, tweets and TV shows. Here are some of the best.

BRILLIANT BOOKS:
1,339 QI Facts to Make Your Jaw Drop - Kindle Edition by John Lloyd and John Mitchinson (Faber and Faber, 2013)
Guinness World Records (Guinness World Records, 2013)
Knowledge Encyclopedia (Dorling Kindserley, 2013)
Ripley's Believe It Or Not 2014 by Ripley Publishing (Random House, 2013)
Stop The Clock by Tom Jackson (Red Lemon Press, 2013)
The 'How It Works' Book of Junior Science (Imagine Publishing, 2013)
The 'How It Works' Book of Amazing Answers to Curious Questions - Kindle Edition (Imagine Publishing, 2013)
1,227 QI Facts to Blow Your Socks Off - Kindle Edition by John Lloyd and John Mitchinson (Faber and Faber, 2012).
5,000 Awesome Facts (About Everything) (National Geographic, 2012)
Extreme Planet (Lonely Planet, 2012)
The Big Book of Knowledge (Parragon, 2010)
Children's Encyclopedia of Animals (Dorling Kindersley, 2009)
How Much Poo Does An Elephant Do? by Mitchell Symons (Red Fox, 2009)
Why Is Snot Green? by Glenn Murphy (Macmillan Children's Books/Science Museum, 2007)

PLUS... the 'QI' TV show and the 'QI Elves' on Twitter
AND... The Horrible Science books

WONDERFUL WEBSITES:
www.britannica.com
www.guinnessworldrecords.com
http://qi.com
www.newscientist.com
www.lookandlearn.com
http://kids.britannica.com
www.nationalgeographic.com
http://uber-facts.com
www.nasa.gov
www.technologyreview.com

SUPER NEWS WEBSITES:
www.bbc.co.uk/news
http://edition.cnn.com

Newspaper websites to look up:
The Guardian, The Independent, The Huffington Post, The Telegraph, and The Daily Mail.

And, of course, there's always the EPIC power of 'Google'.

For a full list of all sources and references used, visit: http://goo.gl/YVEAWk